NORTH AMERICAN ANIMALS

MOOSE

by Megan Borgert-Spaniol

BLASTOFF! READERS 3

BELLWETHER MEDIA • MINNEAPOLIS, MN

Note to Librarians, Teachers, and Parents:

Blastoff! Readers are carefully developed by literacy experts and combine standards-based content with developmentally appropriate text.

Level 1 provides the most support through repetition of high-frequency words, light text, predictable sentence patterns, and strong visual support.

Level 2 offers early readers a bit more challenge through varied simple sentences, increased text load, and less repetition of high-frequency words.

Level 3 advances early-fluent readers toward fluency through increased text and concept load, less reliance on visuals, longer sentences, and more literary language.

Level 4 builds reading stamina by providing more text per page, increased use of punctuation, greater variation in sentence patterns, and increasingly challenging vocabulary.

Level 5 encourages children to move from "learning to read" to "reading to learn" by providing even more text, varied writing styles, and less familiar topics.

Whichever book is right for your reader, Blastoff! Readers are the perfect books to build confidence and encourage a love of reading that will last a lifetime!

This edition first published in 2016 by Bellwether Media, Inc.

No part of this publication may be reproduced in whole or in part without written permission of the publisher. For information regarding permission, write to Bellwether Media, Inc., Attention: Permissions Department, 5357 Penn Avenue South, Minneapolis, MN 55419.

Library of Congress Cataloging-in-Publication Data

Borgert-Spaniol, Megan, 1989- author.
 Moose / by Megan Borgert-Spaniol.
   pages cm. – (Blastoff! Readers. North American Animals)
 Summary: "Simple text and full-color photography introduce beginning readers to moose. Developed by literacy experts for students in kindergarten through third grade"– Provided by publisher.
 Audience: Ages 5-8
 Audience: K to grade 3
 Includes bibliographical references and index.
 ISBN 978-1-62617-260-9 (hardcover: alk. paper)
 1. Moose–Juvenile literature. I. Title.
 QL737.U55B6375 2016
 599.65'7–dc23
                                        2015000510

Printed in the United States of America, North Mankato, MN.

Table of Contents

What Are Moose?	4
Summer and Winter	12
Antlers	14
Calves	18
Glossary	22
To Learn More	23
Index	24

What Are Moose?

Moose are hoofed **mammals**. They are found throughout Canada and the northern United States.

In the Wild

N W E S

Extinct

Extinct in the Wild

Critically Endangered

Endangered

Vulnerable

Near Threatened

Least Concern

moose range =

conservation status: least concern

They live in forests near lakes, ponds, or wetlands.

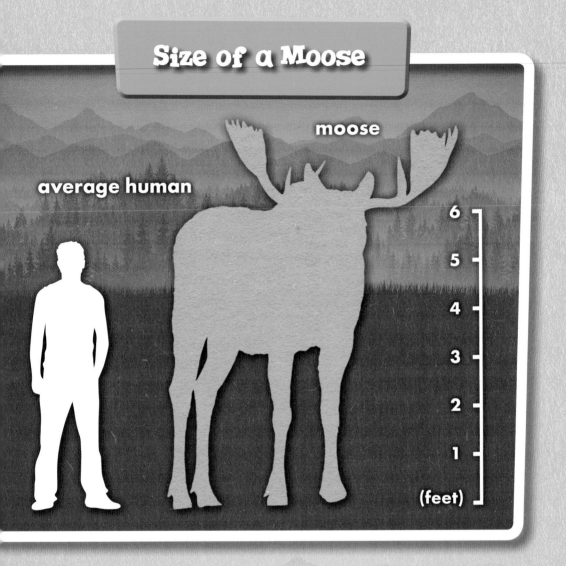

Size of a Moose

average human

moose

6
5
4
3
2
1
(feet)

Moose are the largest members of the deer family. They stand up to 6.5 feet (2 meters) tall from feet to shoulders.

A flap of skin hangs from their throats. It is called a bell.

Male moose are called **bulls**.
Females are **cows**.

Bulls are heavier than cows. They can weigh more than 1,500 pounds (680 kilograms)!

Moose are **herbivores**. They eat leaves, twigs, bark, and buds.

birch bark

dogwood

pinecones

yellow water lilies

They also feed on **aquatic** plants. Duckweed is one favorite.

Summer and Winter

Moose **wade** to cool off in summer. They can swim for several miles at a time.

Identify a Moose

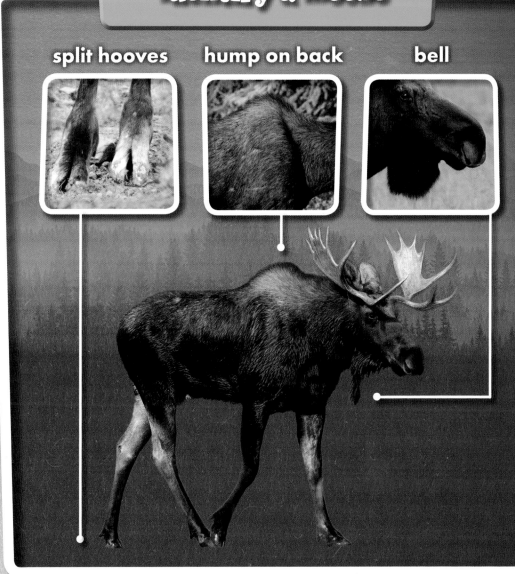

split hooves

hump on back

bell

Long, **hollow** hairs keep moose warm during winter. **Split hooves** help them walk over deep snow.

Bulls have large antlers. These branched bones can measure 6 feet (1.8 meters) wide!

In fall, bulls use their antlers to fight for cows. They lock them together and push. Their thick skin protects them from cuts.

The antlers fall off each winter.

In spring, new antlers start to grow. They are covered in **velvet**.

Calves

A cow gives birth in spring. Her **calf** is reddish brown. She **nurses** her calf for six months.

Baby Facts

Name for babies:	calves
Size of litter:	1 or 2 calves
Length of pregnancy:	8 months
Time spent with mom:	about 1 year

Animals to Avoid

gray wolves

grizzly bears

black bears

mountain lions

The mother moose listens for wolves, bears, and other **predators**. She will charge if they come too close to her young!

Glossary

aquatic—growing in water

bulls—male moose

calf—a baby moose

cows—female moose

herbivores—animals that only eat plants

hollow—empty through the middle; a moose's hollow hairs trap air to keep it warm.

mammals—warm-blooded animals that have backbones and feed their young milk

nurses—feeds milk to her young

predators—animals that hunt other animals for food

split hooves—hooves that are split into two toes; hooves are hard coverings that protect the feet of some animals.

velvet—the fuzzy skin that covers a bull's antlers; the velvet falls off as the antlers grow.

wade—to walk through water

To Learn More

AT THE LIBRARY

Arnold, Caroline. *A Moose's World*. Minneapolis, Minn.: Picture Window Books, 2010.

Macken, JoAnn Early. *Moose*. Pleasantville, N.Y.: Gareth Stevens Pub., 2010.

Numeroff, Laura Joffe. *If You Give a Moose a Muffin*. New York, N.Y.: HarperCollins, 1991.

ON THE WEB

Learning more about moose is as easy as 1, 2, 3.

1. Go to www.factsurfer.com.

2. Enter "moose" into the search box.

3. Click the "Surf" button and you will see a list of related web sites.

With factsurfer.com, finding more information is just a click away.

Index

antlers, 14, 15, 16, 17

bell, 7, 13

bulls, 8, 9, 14, 15

calf, 18, 19

Canada, 4

cows, 8, 9, 15, 18

fight, 15

food, 10, 11

forests, 5

hairs, 13

herbivores, 10

hooves, 4, 13

hump, 13

lakes, 5

mammals, 4

nurses, 18

ponds, 5

predators, 20, 21

range, 4, 5

seasons, 12, 13, 15, 16, 17, 18

size, 6, 9, 14

swim, 12

United States, 4

velvet, 17

wade, 12

wetlands, 5

The images in this book are reproduced through the courtesy of: Don Johnston/ All Canada Photos/ Superstock, front cover; BGSmith, pp. 4-5, 13 (top left, top middle); Teri Virbickis, p. 7; M. Watson/ ardea.c/ Age Fotostock, pp. 8-9; Malgorzata Litkowska, pp. 10-11; Valentina Razumova, p. 11 (top left); Le Do, p. 11 (top right); de2marco, p. 11 (bottom left); KENG MERRY MIKEY MELODY, p. 11 (bottom right); Kirkgeisler, p. 12; Agustin Esmoris, p. 13 (top right); Wesley Aston, p. 13 (bottom); Paul Tessier, p. 14; Yva Momatiuk & John Eastcott/ Corbis, pp. 14-15; Matthew Jacques, p. 16; Wildnerdpix, p. 17; ARCO/ Henry, P./ Glow Images, pp. 18-19; Christophe Avril, p. 19; Maxim Kulko, p. 20 (top left); Nagel Photography, p. 20 (top right); vblinov, p. 20 (bottom left); Ultrashock, p. 20 (bottom right); Ray Bulson/ AlaskaStock/ Corbis, pp. 20-21.